WOMEN'S PROFESSIONAL BASKETBALL

Teamwork:

The

LOS ANGELES SPARKS

in Action

Thomas S. Owens
Diana Star Helmer

The Rosen Publishing Group's
PowerKids Press™
New York

To everyone who has waited or worked for a dream. Here's proof that dreams come true.

Published in 1999 by The Rosen Publishing Group, Inc.
29 East 21st Street, New York, NY 10010

First Edition

Book Design: Michael de Guzman

Photo Credits: p. 4 © Tim O'Dell/WNBA Enterprises, LLC; p. 7 © Reuters/John Kuntz/Archive Photos; p. 8 © Norm Perdue/WNBA Enterprises, LLC, (inset) © Andy Hayt/WNBA Enterprises, LLC; p. 11 © Greg Shamus/WNBA Enterprises, LLC; pp. 12, 20 © Nathaniel S. Butler/WNBA Enterprises, LLC; pp. 15, 21 © Andrew D. Bernstein/WNBA Enterprises, LLC; p. 16 © Noren Trotman/WNBA Enterprises, LLC; p. 19 © Sandy Tenuto/WNBA Enterprises, LLC.

Owens, Tom, 1960-
    Teamwork: the Los Angeles Sparks in action / Thomas S. Owens, Diana Star Helmer.
        p.   cm. — (Women's professional basketball)
    Includes index.
    Summary: Profiles some of the key players on the Los Angeles Sparks professional women's basketball team and describes the team's first year in the WNBA.
    ISBN 0-8239-5240-1
    1. Los Angeles Sparks (Basketball team)—Juvenile literature. 2. Basketball for women—United States—Juvenile literature.
[1. Los Angeles Sparks (Basketball team). 2. Women basketball players. 3. Basketball players.] I. Helmer, Diana Star, 1962-
II. Title. III. Series: Owens, Tom, 1960- Women's professional basketball.
GV885.52.L65O94 1998
796.323'64'0979494—dc21
                          98-16492
                          CIP
                          AC

Contents

Playing Together

The Los Angeles Sparks had lost four of their last five games. All the players had won games before when they were on different teams. Now they were wondering why they couldn't win games together. Finally, the team owners decided to get a new head coach. **Assistant** (uh-SIS-tent) coach Julie Rousseau took over as head coach just hours before the Sparks' next game. By half-time the Sparks had a twenty point lead against the mighty Houston Comets. The Sparks won 77 to 52! Coach Rousseau said "It was beautiful basketball to watch."

◁ New coach Julie Rousseau wanted her players to talk to each other during games to play better.

Sisters of the NBA

   The National Basketball Association (NBA) created the Women's National Basketball Association (WNBA). They decided that the women's teams would play in the same cities as the men's teams while the men were on summer vacation.

   The idea for the WNBA began in 1996 when the Olympics were held in the United States. The U.S. Women's Basketball Team traveled across America, meeting fans. When the women's team won the Olympic gold medal, fans felt like they were cheering for friends. Los Angeles fans cheered even more when the WNBA **league** (LEEG) put one of its first eight teams in their city.

Lisa Leslie, who made the United States proud in the 1996 Olympics, now makes the LA Sparks proud. ▶

Atlanta

Tall and Proud

Lisa Leslie was famous before she joined the WNBA. In high school, college, and at the 1996 Olympics, she was one of the United States' best basketball players. Then she became a model for magazines and TV. At 6 feet 5 inches tall, Lisa is taller than most people. When she was younger, kids at her school used to tease her because she was much taller than everyone else. But Lisa's mother taught Lisa to walk tall and be proud of herself. Lisa is proud. And she chose the Sparks as her team so she could live close to her mother.

◁ Some people thought women basketball players couldn't slam dunk. But Lisa Leslie can!

Lucky Penny

For many years the United States had no **professional** (proh-FEH-shuh-nul) women's sports teams. Some players, such as Penny Toler, played for money and prizes in Italy, Israel, and Greece. Then Penny went to California to join the WNBA. She wanted to be in California because that's where she went to college. On June 21, 1997, Penny was the first player to score points for the WNBA. "When you get older, I think you become better," she says. "You get smarter."

Penny Toler is famous for her flashy ball handling—between her legs and behind her back. ▷

Teamwork

American athletes often play overseas. But no Chinese basketball player ever played in another country until Zheng Haixia came to Los Angeles. In China, "I was always the center of the action," Zheng says. At 6 feet 8 inches tall, Zheng is a great shooter! But running and jumping quickly can be hard for such a big person. With the Sparks, Zheng learned teamwork. A **translator** (TRANZ-lay-ter) helps her speak to her teammates about better ways to work together. Zheng worked so well with her teammates that coaches and sports writers awarded her the first WNBA **Sportsmanship** (SPORTS-min-ship) Award.

◀ In Chinese, Zheng Haixia's name means "Rosy Clouds Over the Sea."

Heidi

Heidi Burge played professional basketball in Greece. But the WNBA didn't **draft** (DRAFT) her. So Heidi asked if she could just practice with the Sparks. When manager Rhonda Windham saw how well Heidi worked with the team, she asked Heidi to join the Sparks. Heidi felt at home with the tall Sparks players. She and her sister, Heather, are the tallest **identical** (eye-DEN-tih-kul) twins in the world! Each sister is 6 feet 5 inches tall. Heather played professional basketball overseas too. She cheers at Heidi's games. The twins hope they both will get to play in the WNBA someday.

Because they are the tallest identical twins in the world, Heidi (shown here) and Heather Burge are in the *Guiness Book of World Records*. ▷

The New Assistant

When Julie Rousseau became the Sparks head coach, they had to hire a new assistant coach. Orlando Woolridge became the assistant. Orlando had played for the NBA's Los Angeles Lakers. Orlando wasn't a Lakers **starter** (STAR-ter). When he wasn't playing, he watched his team. By watching, Orlando saw how players could work better together. That's what he does for the Sparks. "It's still about basketball," Orlando says.

Assistant coach Orlando Woolridge coached high school and college girls basketball before becoming the Sparks' "big brother."

The Last Game

The Sparks were in Phoenix on August 24, 1997, the last game of the WNBA season. Winning could mean going to the first-ever WNBA play-offs. Losing would mean going home. The game was tied with 25 seconds left. Phoenix stole the Sparks' ball—but missed their shot. So the game went into **overtime** (OH-ver-tym). Soon the Sparks fell behind, 71 to 64. Then Penny Toler got one basket, then another! Even though they tried their hardest, the Sparks lost the game. The Sparks ended the season with fourteen wins and fourteen losses.

Penny Toler and her teammates worked their hardest in the last game against the Mercury. ▷

ALL-WNBA TEAM

A Team of Winners

Even when the Sparks lost, their fans made the team feel like winners. Twenty Sparks fans drove all day to watch the last Sparks game in Phoenix. More than 1,000 fans came to watch the team practice one day. Players can always be winners, even when their team loses. Lisa Leslie was named to the All-WNBA **First Team** (FERST TEEM). She was the league's best in **rebounds** (REE-bowndz), second in blocking, and third in points. Zheng Haixia was first in the league in **field goals** (FEELD GOHLZ). Penny Toler was second in assists.

◁ The Sparks' games were shown on TV more than any other WNBA team.

The Sparks' Future

The first WNBA season was over. But the WNBA league was just beginning. The next year, two new teams would be added, one in Washington, DC, and another in Detroit, Michigan. More games will be added to the season and to the play-offs. Teams in next year's semi-final and final rounds will get more chances to win these important games. Many Sparks players went overseas to play professionally during their vacation. They knew this would help them be ready for the new WNBA year, and make the Sparks better than ever.

Web Sites:

You can learn more about women's professional basketball at these Web sites:

http://www.wnba.com
http://www.fullcourt.com

Glossary

assistant (uh-SIS-tent) Someone who helps.

draft (DRAFT) When teams pick players from colleges or other leagues to play on their team.

field goal (FEELD GOHL) When a ball goes through the hoop for two points.

First Team (FERST TEEM) An imaginary "dream team" made up of the best players in the league.

identical (eye-DEN-tih-kul) To be alike in every way.

league (LEEG) A group of teams who play against each other in the same sport.

overtime (OH-ver-tym) Extra playing time after a game to resolve a tie.

professional (proh-FEH-shuh-nul) An athlete who earns money for playing a sport.

rebound (REE-bownd) To get control of the ball after a missed shot.

sportsmanship (SPORTS-min-ship) The fair way in which athletes play a game and treat other players.

starter (STAR-ter) Someone who plays for most of a game, starting right from the beginning.

translator (TRANZ-lay-ter) A person who can listen to someone speak in one language and then tell someone else what the person said in a different language.

Index

DATE DUE			